THE CALL OF THE WILD

Jack London

TECHNICAL DIRECTOR Maxwell Krohn
EDITORIAL DIRECTOR Justin Kestler
MANAGING EDITOR Ben Florman

SERIES EDITORS Boomie Aglietti, Justin Kestler
PRODUCTION Christian Lorentzen

WRITERS Debra Grossman, Ross Douthat
EDITORS Dennis Quinio, Benjamin Morgan

This edition published by Spark Publishing

Spark Publishing
A Division of SparkNotes LLC
120 Fifth Avenue, 8th Floor
New York, NY 10011

02 03 04 05 SN 9 8 7 6 5 4 3 2 1

Please send all comments and questions or report errors to
feedback@sparknotes.com.

Library of Congress information available upon request

Printed and bound in the United States

RRD-C

ISBN 1-58663-439-9

INTRODUCTION: STOPPING TO BUY SPARKNOTES ON A SNOWY EVENING

Whose words these are you *think* you know.
Your paper's due tomorrow, though;
We're glad to see you stopping here
To get some help before you go.

Lost your course? You'll find it here.
Face tests and essays without fear.
Between the words, good grades at stake:
Get great results throughout the year.

Once school bells caused your heart to quake
As teachers circled each mistake.
Use SparkNotes and no longer weep,
Ace every single test you take.

Yes, books are lovely, dark, and deep,
But only what you grasp you keep,
With hours to go before you sleep,
With hours to go before you sleep.

CONTENTS

CONTEXT

J ACK LONDON WAS BORN in San Francisco on January 12, 1876, the illegitimate son of Flora Wellman, the rebellious daughter of an aristocratic family, and William Chaney, a traveling astrologer who abandoned Flora when she became pregnant. Eight months after her son was born, Flora married John London, a grocer and Civil War veteran whose last name the infant took. London grew up in Oakland, and his family was mired in poverty throughout his youth. He remained in school only through the eighth grade but was a voracious reader and a frequent visitor to the Oakland Public Library, where he went about educating himself and laying the groundwork for his impending literary career.

In his adolescent years, London led a rough life, spending time as a pirate in San Francisco Bay, traveling the Far East on sealing expeditions, and making his way across America as a tramp. Finally, temporarily tired of adventure, London returned to Oakland and graduated from high school. He was even admitted to the University of California at Berkeley, but he stayed only for a semester. The Klondike gold rush (in Canada's Yukon Territory) had begun, and in 1897 London left college to seek his fortune in the snowy North.

The gold rush did not make London rich, but it furnished him with plenty of material for his career as a writer, which began in the late 1890s and continued until his death in 1916. He worked as a reporter, covering the Russo-Japanese War of 1904 and the Mexican Revolution in the 1910s; meanwhile, he published over fifty books and became, at the time, America's most famous author. For a while, he was one of the most widely read authors in the world. He embodied, it was said, the spirit of the American West, and his portrayal of adventure and frontier life seemed like a breath of fresh air in comparison with nineteenth-century Victorian fiction, which was often overly concerned with what had begun to seem like trivial and irrelevant social norms.

The Call of the Wild, published in 1903, remains London's most famous work, blending his experiences as a gold prospector in the Canadian wilderness with his ideas about nature and the struggle for existence. He drew these ideas from various influential figures, including Charles Darwin, an English naturalist credited with developing theories about biological evolution, and Friedrich Nietzsche, a prominent German philosopher. Although *The Call of the Wild* is first and foremost a story about a dog, it displays a philosophical depth absent in most animal adventures.

London was married twice—once in 1900, to his math tutor and friend Bess Maddern, and again in 1905, to his secretary Charmian Kittredge, whom he considered his true love. As his works soared in popularity, he became a contradictory figure, arguing for socialist principles and women's rights even as he himself lived a materialist life of luxury, sailing the world in his boat, the *Snark,* and running a large ranch in northern California. Meanwhile, he preached equality and the brotherhood of man, even as novels like *The Call of the Wild* celebrated violence, power, and brute force.

London died young, on November 22, 1916. He had been plagued by stomach problems and failing kidneys for years, but many have suggested that his death was a suicide. Whatever the cause, it is clear that London, who played the various roles of journalist, novelist, prospector, sailor, pirate, husband, and father, lived life to the fullest.

PLOT OVERVIEW

BUCK, A POWERFUL DOG, half St. Bernard and half sheep-dog, lives on Judge Miller's estate in California's Santa Clara Valley. He leads a comfortable life there, but it comes to an end when men discover gold in the Klondike region of Canada and a great demand arises for strong dogs to pull sleds. Buck is kidnapped by a gardener on the Miller estate and sold to dog traders, who teach Buck to obey by beating him with a club and, subsequently, ship him north to the Klondike.

Arriving in the chilly North, Buck is amazed by the cruelty he sees around him. As soon as another dog from his ship, Curly, gets off the boat, a pack of huskies violently attacks and kills her. Watching her death, Buck vows never to let the same fate befall him. Buck becomes the property of Francois and Perrault, two mail carriers working for the Canadian government, and begins to adjust to life as a sled dog. He recovers the instincts of his wild ancestors: he learns to fight, scavenge for food, and sleep beneath the snow on winter nights. At the same time, he develops a fierce rivalry with Spitz, the lead dog in the team. One of their fights is broken up when a pack of wild dogs invades the camp, but Buck begins to undercut Spitz's authority, and eventually the two dogs become involved in a major fight. Buck kills Spitz and takes his place as the lead dog.

With Buck at the head of the team, Francois and Perrault's sled makes record time. However, the men soon turn the team over to a mail carrier who forces the dogs to carry much heavier loads. In the midst of a particularly arduous trip, one of the dogs becomes ill, and eventually the driver has to shoot him. At the end of this journey, the dogs are exhausted, and the mail carrier sells them to a group of American gold hunters—Hal, Charles, and Mercedes.

Buck's new masters are inexperienced and out of place in the wilderness. They overload the sled, beat the dogs, and plan poorly. Halfway through their journey, they begin to run out of food. While the humans bicker, the dogs begin to starve, and the weaker animals soon die. Of an original team of fourteen, only five are still alive when they limp into John Thornton's camp, still some distance from their destination. Thornton warns them that the ice over which they are traveling is melting and that they may fall through it. Hal dismisses these warnings and tries to get going immediately. The other dogs begin to move, but Buck refuses. When Hal begins to beat him, Thornton intervenes, knocking a knife from Hal's hand and cutting Buck loose. Hal curses Thornton and starts the sled again, but before they have gone a quarter of a mile, the ice breaks open, swallowing both the humans and the dogs.

Thornton becomes Buck's master, and Buck's devotion to him is total. He saves Thornton from drowning in a river, attacks a man who tries to start a fight with Thornton in a bar, and, most remarkably, wins a $1,600 wager for his new master by pulling a sled carrying a thousand-pound load. But Buck's love for Thornton is mixed with a growing attraction to the wild, and he feels as if he is being called away from civilization and into the wilderness. This feeling grows stronger when he accompanies Thornton and his friends in search of a lost mine hidden deep in the Canadian forest.

While the men search for gold, Buck ranges far afield, befriending wolves and hunting bears and moose. He always returns to Thornton in the end, until, one day, he comes back to camp to find that Yeehat Indians have attacked and killed his master. Buck attacks the Indians, killing several and scattering the rest, and then heads off into the wild, where he becomes the leader of a pack of wolves. He becomes a legendary figure, a Ghost Dog, fathering countless cubs and inspiring fear in the Yeehats—but every year he returns to the place where Thornton died, to mourn his master before returning to his life in the wild.

CHARACTER LIST

Buck   A powerful dog, half St. Bernard and half sheepdog, who is stolen from a California estate and sold as a sled dog in the Arctic. Buck gradually evolves from a pampered pet into a fierce, masterful animal, able to hold his own in the cruel, kill-or-be-killed world of the North. Though he loves his final master, John Thornton, he feels the wild calling him away from civilization and longs to reconnect with the primitive roots of his species.

John Thornton Buck's final master, a gold hunter experienced in the ways of the Klondike. Thornton saves Buck from death at the hands of Hal, and Buck rewards Thornton with fierce loyalty. Thornton's relationship to Buck is the ideal man-dog relationship: each guards the other's back and is completely devoted to the other. The strength of their bond is enough to keep Buck from acting on the forces he feels are calling him into the wild.

Spitz   Buck's archrival and the original leader of Francois's dog team. Spitz is a fierce animal—a "devil-dog," one man calls him—who is used to fighting with other dogs and winning. He meets his match in Buck, however, who is as strong as Spitz and possesses more cunning. Spitz is an amoral being who fights for survival with all of his might, disregarding what is right and wrong.

Francois A French Canadian mail driver who buys Buck and adds him to his team. Francois is an experienced man, accustomed to life in the North, and he impresses Buck with his fairness and good sense.

Perrault   A French Canadian who, together with Francois, turns Buck into a sled dog for the Canadian government. Both Perrault and Francois speak in heavily accented English, which London distinguishes from the rest of the novel's dialogue.

Hal   An American gold seeker, Hal comes to Canada with his sister, Mercedes, and her husband, Charles, in search of adventure and riches. The three buy Buck and his team and try to drive them, but their inexperience makes them terrible masters, as they run out of food during the journey and bicker among themselves. Hal and his companions are meant to represent the weakness of overcivilized men and to embody the man-dog relationship at its worst.

Mercedes   Charles's wife and Hal's sister. Mercedes is spoiled and pampered, and her unreasonable demands slow her, Hal, and Charles on their journey and contribute to its disastrous ending. Her civilized manner, however, contrasts that of her unprepared brother and husband in that she initially feels sympathetic for the worn-out sled team. Her behavior, London suggests, demonstrates how civilized women are unsuited for life in the wild, having been spoiled and babied by the men around them.

Charles   Hal's brother-in-law and Mercedes' husband. Charles shares their inexperience and folly.

Dave   A dog on Buck's team. Dave becomes ill on one of the team's journeys but refuses to leave the harness, preferring to die pulling the sled. In his stubbornness at this task, Dave is an example of gritty determination.

Sol-leks   An older, more experienced dog on Buck's team.

Curly   A friend of Buck's, met on the journey to the North. Curly's death, when she naively tries to be friendly to a husky, acts as a warning to Buck of the harshness and cruelty of his new home.

Judge Miller Buck's original master, the owner of a large estate in California's Santa Clara Valley.

Manuel   A gardener's helper on Judge Miller's estate. Manuel kidnaps Buck and sells him in order to pay off his gambling debts.

CHARACTER LIST

ANALYSIS OF MAJOR CHARACTERS

BUCK

Although *The Call of the Wild* is told from the perspective of an anonymous third-person narrator, the events that are recounted are those that the dog Buck experiences directly. As such, it is not unreasonable to call him the only fully developed character in the story. He is the only character whose past we know anything about, and London is careful to emphasize the human qualities of his protagonist, enabling us to empathize with the animal. Filtered through the third-person omniscience of the narrator, Buck comes across as far more than a creature of instinct, since he has a sense of wonder, shame, and justice. He also possesses a capacity for mystical experiences and for great, unselfish love, as his relationship to Thornton amply demonstrates. He may be a dog, but he is more human than many of the people around him.

Buck's story is cyclical: he is introduced as a pampered prince, and the story concludes with Buck as a veritable king of beasts. In between, Buck undergoes experiences that provide him with greater insight about the world. Buck begins as a spoiled regent, strutting proudly over his soft, sun-kissed domain, but he abruptly sees everything taken away from him. He is reduced to nothing, beaten and kicked and forced to pull sleds through the Canadian wilderness. This experience, though, far from destroying him, makes him stronger, and he wins back his kingdom—or rather, he wins a new kingdom, a wild one that better suits his true destiny as a wild animal. *The Call of the Wild* is, as its title suggests, a celebration of wildness, of primitive life, and even of savagery. Buck's rise to greatness is not an easy path; it is a struggle, a course strewn with obstacles, from the long duel with his rival Spitz to the folly of Hal, Mercedes, and Charles. But these obstacles, London indicates, are to be rejoiced in rather than avoided: life is ultimately a long struggle for mastery, and the greatest dogs (or men), the Bucks of the world, will always seek out struggles in order to prove their greatness. Thus, when Buck goes from being a moral, civilized pet to a fierce, bloodthirsty, vio-

CHARACTER ANALYSIS

lent wolf-dog, we are glad rather than shocked, because we know that he is fulfilling his highest possible destiny.

JOHN THORNTON

The Call of the Wild is, first and foremost, the story of Buck's gradual transformation from a tame beast into a wild animal. But even as the novel celebrates the life of a wild creature, it presents us with the character of John Thornton, whose connection to Buck suggests that there may be something good and natural in the human-dog relationship, despite its flaws. Thornton, a seasoned gold prospector, saves Buck from being beaten to death by the odious Hal and then becomes Buck's master. From then on, a deep and abiding love blossoms between man and dog. Their relationship is a reciprocal one—Thornton saves Buck, and Buck later saves Thornton from drowning in a river. It is clear that Buck is more of a partner than a servant to the prospector. This mutual respect, we are assured, is characteristic of all Thornton's relationships to dogs—every one of his animals bears an abiding love for him, which is returned in kind. Even as Buck is increasingly drawn to a life away from humanity, a life in the wild, his affection for Thornton keeps him from making the final break. Indeed, so strong is their bond that it is broken only when Thornton dies, and even then Buck makes an annual pilgrimage to his last master's final resting place.

Buck is prone to visions of more primitive worlds, and sometimes he sees the humans around him as ancient men, wearing animal skins and living in caves or trees. In some of these visions, he is running alongside these men, protecting them from the terrors of the night. His relationship to Thornton, the novel implies, is like these ancient man-dog connections; it is primitive rather than civilized, and so it remains strong even as Buck leaves the civilized world behind.

HAL, CHARLES, AND MERCEDES

These three can be analyzed in a group, because London never develops them beyond our initial impressions of them, which are strikingly similar: Hal and Charles are foolish and callow; Mercedes is spoiled and sentimental. Taken together, the trio serves as a vehicle through which London attacks the debilitating effects of human civilization and warns of how little use such civilization is in the wild. From their first appearance, Hal, Charles, and Mercedes are woefully out of place in the untamed North. Both Hal and Charles display "a callowness sheer and unutterable," while Mercedes is spoiled and unreasonable—"it was her custom to be helpless," London notes. As a group, the three have no experience in the wild, and, thus, they make mistake after mistake, overpacking the sled, allowing Mercedes to ride instead of walking, and miscalculating how much food they need for the journey to Dawson. When their mistakes become apparent, instead of taking action, they begin bickering and feuding, fighting over old grudges and trifles rather than dealing with the problems at hand.

The civilized world tolerates and even smiles on such absurdity, London suggests, but the wild has no such mercy. In the cold of the Klondike, incompetence is deadly, not only for the three foolish Americans but also for the team of dogs, for the humans' poor planning has brought them to the brink of starvation. Hal, Charles, and Mercedes are weak and foolish figures, and their folly has its own reward—death in the icy waters of a northern river.

THEMES, MOTIFS & SYMBOLS

THEMES

Themes are the fundamental and often universal ideas explored in a literary work.

THE INDISPENSABLE STRUGGLE FOR MASTERY

The Call of the Wild is a story of transformation in which the old Buck—the civilized, moral Buck—must adjust to the harsher realities of life in the frosty North, where survival is the only imperative. Kill or be killed is the only morality among the dogs of the Klondike, as Buck realizes from the moment he steps off the boat and watches the violent death of his friend Curly. The wilderness is a cruel, uncaring world, where only the strong prosper. It is, one might say, a perfect Darwinian world, and London's depiction of it owes much to Charles Darwin, who proposed the theory of evolution to explain the development of life on Earth and envisioned a natural world defined by fierce competition for scarce resources. The term often used to describe Darwin's theory, although he did not coin it, is "the survival of the fittest," a phrase that describes Buck's experience perfectly. In the old, warmer world, he might have sacrificed his life out of moral considerations; now, however, he abandons any such considerations in order to survive.

But London is not content to make the struggle for survival the central theme of his novel; instead, his protagonist struggles toward a higher end, namely mastery. We see this struggle particularly in Buck's conflict with Spitz, in his determination to become the lead dog on Francois and Perrault's team, and, at the end of the novel, in the way that he battles his way to the leadership of the wolf pack. Buck does not merely want to survive; he wants to dominate—as do his rivals, dogs like Spitz. In this quest for domination, which is celebrated by London's narrative, we can observe the influence of Friedrich Nietzsche, a German philosopher of the late nineteenth century. Nietzsche's worldview held that the world was composed of masters, those who possessed what he called "the will to power,"

THEMES

and slaves, those who did not possess this will. Nietzsche delighted in using animal metaphors, comparing masters to "birds of prey" and "blonde beasts" and comparing slaves to sheep and other herd animals. London's Buck, with his indomitable strength and fierce desire for mastery, is a canine version of Nietzsche's masterful men, his Napoleon Bonapartes and Julius Caesars. Buck is a savage creature, in a sense, and hardly a moral one, but London, like Nietzsche, expects us to applaud this ferocity. His novel suggests that there is no higher destiny for man or beast than to struggle, and win, in the battle for mastery.

THE POWER OF ANCESTRAL MEMORY AND PRIMITIVE INSTINCTS

When Buck enters the wild, he must learn countless lessons in order to survive, and he learns them well. But the novel suggests that his success in the frozen North is not merely a matter of *learning* the ways of the wild; rather, Buck gradually *recovers* primitive instincts and memories that his wild ancestors possessed, which have been buried as dogs have become civilized creatures. The technical term for what happens to Buck is atavism—the reappearance in a modern creature of traits that defined its remote forebears. London returns to this theme again and again, constantly reminding us that Buck is "retrogressing," as the novel puts it, into a wilder way of life that all dogs once shared. "He was older than the days he had seen and the breaths he had drawn," we are told. "He linked the past with the present, and the eternity behind him throbbed through him in a mighty rhythm to which he swayed as the tides and seasons swayed." Buck even has occasional visions of this older world, when humans wore animal skins and lived in caves, and when wild dogs hunted their prey in the primeval forests. His connection to his ancestral identity is thus more than instinctual; it is mystical. The civilized world, which seems so strong, turns out to be nothing more than a thin veneer, which is quickly worn away to reveal the ancient instincts lying dormant underneath. Buck hears the call of the wild, and London implies that, in the right circumstances, we might hear it too.

THE LAWS OF CIVILIZATION AND OF WILDERNESS

While the two lives that Buck leads stand in stark contrast to each other, this contrast does not go unchallenged throughout the novel. His life with Judge Miller is leisurely, calm, and unchallenging, while his transition to the wilderness shows him a life that is savage, frenetic, and demanding. While it would be tempting to assume that these two lives are polar opposites, events later in the novel show some ways in which both the wild and civilization have underlying social codes, hierarchies, and even laws. For example, the pack that Buck joins is not anarchic; the position of lead dog is coveted and given to the most powerful dog. The lead dog takes responsibility for group decisions and has a distinctive style of leadership; the main factor in the rivalry between Buck and Spitz is that Buck sides with the less popular, marginal dogs instead of the stronger ones. Buck, then, advocates the rights of a minority in the pack—a position that is strikingly similar to that of his original owner, the judge, who is the novel's most prominent example of civilization.

The rules of the civilized and uncivilized worlds are, of course, extremely different—in the wild, many conflicts are resolved through bloody fights rather than through reasoned mediation. But the novel suggests that what is important in both worlds is to understand and abide by the rules which that world has set up, and it is only when those rules are broken that we see true savagery and disrespect for life. Mercedes, Hal, and Charles enter the wild with little understanding of the rules one must follow to become integrated and survive. Their inability to ration food correctly, their reliance upon their largely useless knife and gun, and their disregard for the dogs' suffering all attest to laws of the wilderness that they misunderstand or choose to ignore. As a result, the wilderness institutes a natural consequence for their actions. Precisely because they do not heed the warnings that the wild provides via one of its residents, John Thornton, they force the team over unstable ice and fall through to their deaths. The novel seems to say that the wild does not allow chaos or wanton behavior but instead institutes a strict social and natural order different from, but not inferior to, that of the civilized world.

THE MEMBERSHIP OF THE INDIVIDUAL IN THE GROUP

When Buck arrives in the wild, his primordial instincts do not awaken immediately, and he requires a great deal of external help before he is suited to life there. Help arrives in realizations about the very different rules that govern the world outside of civilization, but also in the support of the pack of which he becomes a part. Two dogs in particular, Dave and Sol-leks, after having established their seniority, instruct Buck in the intricacies of sled pulling. Furthermore, the group members take pride in their work, even though they are serving men. When they make trips in good time, they congratulate themselves—they all participate in a common enterprise.

At the same time, however, one of the most valued traits in the wilderness is individualism. If *The Call of the Wild* is a story about ultimately achieving mastery over a foreign, primal world, that mastery is achieved only through separation from the group and independent survival. Throughout much of the story, Buck is serving a master or a pack; even as a leader he is carrying out someone else's commands and is responsible for the well-being of the group. In many ways, then, when John Thornton cuts Buck free from his harness, he is also beginning the process of Buck's separation from a pack mentality. Although Buck continues to serve Thornton, his yearnings for a solitary life in the wild eventually overcome him.

The balance between individual and group is disrupted once more, however, toward the end of the novel, when Buck becomes the leader of a wolf pack. Although the pack is much different from the dog pack whose responsibility was to serve humans by pulling sleds, the message seems to be that, while encouraging the skills to survive on one's own, the wild ultimately requires the cooperation of a group in order to ensure individual survival.

MOTIFS

> *Motifs are recurring structures, contrasts, or literary devices that can help to develop and inform the text's major themes.*

VIOLENT STRUGGLE
Life-and-death battles punctuate *The Call of the Wild*'s narrative, serving as reminders of the dangers of life in the Klondike, but more importantly as markers of Buck's gradual integration into his new environment. When Buck first arrives in the north, he watches a friendly dog named Curly brutally killed by a husky. Soon, he finds himself in a rivalry with Spitz that ends with the two of them locked in single combat, a battle from which only Buck emerges alive. Having established himself as a dominant dog with this victory, Buck must continue to prove himself in battles with other creatures—with a bear, with a moose, and, finally, with humans. When Buck kills the Yeehat Indians who have killed John Thornton, he is fighting for his life against mankind for the first time, a sure sign of his final assimilation into the wild.

VISIONS

One of the themes of *The Call of the Wild* is "atavism," or an animal's (in this case, Buck's) recovery of the instincts of his wild ancestors. For Buck, this recovery involves repeated visions of his primitive past, which usually occur late at night when he is lying alongside a campfire. He sees the men around him as primitive men, draped in furs and wary of the prehistoric dark around them, and then he has visions of himself as a primitive, wild creature, hunting his prey in the primeval forests. Each of these visions brings him closer to his destiny, which is the return to his ancestors' ways and becoming a wild animal himself.

SYMBOLS

Symbols are objects, characters, figures, or colors used to represent abstract ideas or concepts.

MERCEDES' POSSESSIONS

Mercedes loads the sled up with so many of her things that the dogs cannot possibly pull it; later, she herself gets on the sled, making the load even heavier. Her insistence on having all of her possessions with her emphasizes the difference between the wild, where the value of an object lies in its immediate usefulness, and civilization, where the value of an object lies in its ability to symbolize the wealth of its possessor. Material possessions and consumerism have no place in the wild, and it is at least partly Mercedes' inability to recognize this fact that leads to her death when the overburdened sled falls through the ice.

BUCK'S TRACES

The significance of Buck's traces—the straps that bind him to the rest of the team—changes as the plot develops. The novel initially charts his descent from his position as the monarch of Judge Miller's place in civilization to a servile status in which it is his duty to pull the sled for humans. But as he becomes more a part of the wild, Buck begins to understand the hierarchy of the pack that pulls the sled, and he begins to gain authority over the pack. After his duel with Spitz, he is harnessed into the lead dog's position; his harness now represents not servitude to the humans but leadership over the dogs. Finally, however, John Thornton cuts Buck free from his traces, an act that symbolizes his freedom from a world in which he serves humans. Now a companion to Thornton rather than a servant, Buck gradually begins to enter a world of individual survival in the wild.

BUCK'S FIRST BEATINGS WITH THE CLUB; CURLY'S DEATH

When Buck is kidnapped, he attempts to attack one of the men who has seized him, only to be beaten repeatedly with a club. This moment, when his fighting spirit is temporarily broken, along with the brutal killing of Curly by a group of vicious sled dogs, symbolizes Buck's departure from the old, comfortable life of a pet in a warm climate, and his entrance into a new world where the only law is "the law of club and fang."

BUCK'S ATTACK ON THE YEEHATS

In the closing chapters of the novel, Buck feels the call of life in the wild drawing him away from mankind, away from campfires and towns, and into the forest. The only thing that prevents him from going, that keeps him tied to the world of men, is his love for John Thornton. When the Yeehat Indians kill Thornton, Buck's last tie to humanity is cut, and he becomes free to attack the Yeehats, killing a number of them. To attack a human being would once have been unthinkable for Buck, and his willingness to do so now symbolizes the fact that his transformation is complete—that he has truly embraced his wild nature.

SYMBOLS

SUMMARY & ANALYSIS

CHAPTER I: *INTO THE PRIMITIVE*

SUMMARY

> *He had a fine pride in himself, was even a trifle*
> *egotistical, as country gentlemen sometimes become*
> *because of their insular situation.*
>
> (See QUOTATIONS, p. 39)

Buck, a large and handsome dog who is part St. Bernard and part Scotch sheep dog, lives on a sizable estate in California's Santa Clara Valley. He is four years old and was born on the estate, which is owned by the wealthy Judge Miller. Buck is the undisputed master of Judge Miller's place, as the locals call it, and is beloved by the Miller children and grandchildren. Buck has the run of the entire place, confident of his superiority to the pampered house pets and the fox terriers that live in the kennels.

But, unbeknownst to Buck, there is a shadow over his happy life. The year is 1897, and men from all over the world are traveling north for the gold rush that has hit the Klondike region of Canada, just east of Alaska. They need strong dogs to pull their sleds on the treacherous journey. Nor does Buck realize that Manuel, a gardener on Judge Miller's estate, is an undesirable acquaintance. Manuel's love of gambling in the Chinese lottery makes it difficult for him to support his wife and several children. One day, while the judge is away, Manuel takes Buck for a walk and leads him to a flag station where a stranger is waiting. Money changes hands, and Manuel ties a rope around Buck's neck. When the rope is tightened, Buck attacks the stranger, but he finds it impossible to break free. The man fights him; Buck's strength fails, and he blacks out and is thrown into the baggage car of the train.

When Buck regains consciousness, he feels himself being jolted around. He hears the whistle of the train and, from having traveled with the judge, recognizes the sensation of riding in a baggage car. He opens his eyes angrily and sees the kidnapper reaching for his throat. He bites the man's hand and is thrown down and choked repeatedly, then locked into a cagelike crate. He stays there for the rest of the night, and, in the morning, his crate is carried out by four men. Buck is passed from vehicle to vehicle, neither eating nor drinking for two days and two nights. He grows angrier and resolves never to let his tormentors tie a rope around his neck again.

In Seattle, Buck's crate is lifted into a small yard with high walls, while a stout man signs for him. Buck decides that this new man is his next tormentor and lunges at him inside the cage. The man smiles and brings out a hatchet and a club. He begins to break the crate, and the other men step back fearfully. Buck snarls and growls and leaps at the man with all his weight, but he feels a blow from the club. It is the first time he has been hit with a club, so he is both hurt and stunned, but he continues trying to attack until the man beats him into submission. Once Buck is exhausted and prostrate, the man brings him water and meat and pats him on the head. Buck understands that he does not stand a chance against a man with a club—it is his introduction into "primitive law," where might makes right.

Buck watches other men arrive, sometimes taking other dogs away with them, and he is glad that he is not chosen. Buck's time finally comes when a French Canadian named Perrault buys him and a Newfoundland bitch named Curly. They are taken onto a ship called the *Narwhal* and turned over to another French Canadian named Francois. They join two other dogs, Spitz and Dave, on the journey northward, and Buck realizes that the weather is growing colder. Finally, they arrive and step out onto a cold surface that Buck does not recognize, never having seen snow before.

> *The facts of life took on a fiercer aspect and . . .*
> *he faced it with all the latent cunning of his*
> *nature aroused.*
>
> (See QUOTATIONS, p. 40)

ANALYSIS

The meaning of chapter titles in *The Call of the Wild* extends beyond a simple description of the plot. The first chapter, "Into the Primitive," is concerned not only with Buck's departure from civilization and his entrance into a more savage, primitive world, but also with the contrast between civilized life and primitive life. This contrast is strong throughout the novel, and the story of Buck's adventures in the Klondike is largely the story of how he gradually sheds all the customs that define his earlier life in human society to become a creature of the wild, primal world of the north. Here, in the first days after his kidnapping, he takes the first steps away from his old life and toward a new one.

As the novel opens, he is clearly a creature of the civilized world, a world defined by gentility, order, and rules, and embodied by Judge Miller's sprawling home in the "sun-kissed" Santa Clara Valley. Furthermore, Buck's original owner is a judge, overseeing the fair rule of law that allows for civilized life. The judge's estate is an "orderly array" of buildings, over which Buck rules almost from birth. Even though the arrangement is orderly, it is not necessarily democratic: Buck never won the right to rule, as he does later in the wild North, but rather inherited it, living the life of a "sated aristocrat." In this world, Buck is a pet rather than a servant; he does not work for or protect Judge Miller but exists as a companion and playmate. There is no struggle in this life, and no burdens that must be borne—there is only luxury and contentment.

Buck's departure "into the primitive" begins to demonstrate a different kind of law, one in which birthright and aristocracy are meaningless. Throughout the novel, London contrasts the rules of the old world that Judge Miller inhabits with the laws of life in the harsh, wild Klondike. Buck learns the first of these laws when the man beats him with the club. "That club," we are told, "was a revelation. It was his introduction to the reign of primitive law." The central feature of that law, of course, is that might makes right— that the use of force is justified by the fact that it prevails over the lack of force or brutality. This philosophy develops throughout the novel, as Buck's life becomes a harsh struggle for existence in which he must either kill or be killed. The club also teaches Buck, for the first time, that human beings can be the enemy, although the full implications of this knowledge remain to be considered.

The novel is told primarily from Buck's point of view, filtered through the third-person omniscience of a narrator, and, although the protagonist of *The Call of the Wild* is a dog, he inspires a very humanlike empathy. London is not simply substituting an animal protagonist for a human one; he is particularly concerned with understanding the parallels between human life and animal life, which seem on the surface to be so different from each other. The novel suggests that, in their most primitive states, both human and animal are defined by a struggle for survival and mastery. In order to allow us to empathize with Buck as an animal narrator and see our own lives reflected in his, London gives his protagonist capacities that are normally reserved for humans. Buck is not merely a creature of instinct but is capable of wonder, concerned about justice, and able to feel shame. He is, much like the human beings who surround him, intensely self-conscious.

CHAPTER II: *THE LAW OF CLUB AND FANG*

SUMMARY

> *Thus, as token of what a puppet thing life is the ancient song surged through him and he came into his own again.*
>
> (See QUOTATIONS, p. 41)

Buck understands that he has been taken from civilization into a wild, primitive place, and his first day in the North is extremely unpleasant. Both the dogs and the men around him are cruel and violent, and Buck is shocked to see the way the wolfish dogs fight. Buck's traveling companion, a female dog named Curly, approaches a husky in a friendly way, but the husky attacks her immediately, ripping her face open. Thirty or forty other huskies approach, and Curly lunges at her assailant. She tumbles off her feet, and the other dogs rush in, trampling her. The men come and fight off the dogs with clubs and an ax. Only two minutes have passed, but Curly is lying dead and bloody on the ground. Buck realizes that to survive in this world, he will have to make sure that he never goes down in a fight. He also decides that he hates Spitz, who seems to be laughing at Curly's fate.

Francois fastens Buck into a harness and sets him to work hauling a sled. Buck finds it to be a humbling experience, as he has seen horses performing such labor before. Nevertheless, he tries his best, responding to Francois's whip and the nips of Dave and the growls of Spitz, deferring to the more experienced sled dogs. Spitz is the team's lead dog, carving a path through the snow. Buck learns quickly and makes good progress. He learns to stop at "ho," to move at "mush," and how to turn and move downhill.

In the afternoon, Perrault brings back two more dogs, Billee and Joe. They are both huskies and are brothers, but they are very different from one another. Billee is excessively good-natured, while Joe is sour. Each of them is confronted by the belligerent Spitz, but while the friendly Billee is easily cowed, Joe snaps back until Spitz leaves him alone. Another dog, Sol-leks, joins them by the evening. He is an old husky with one eye, and he does not like to be approached from his blind side. Buck accidentally approaches him from that side once and gets his shoulder slashed. He avoids making the same mistake again, and the two dogs become friends.

That night, Buck has trouble finding a place to sleep. He tries to enter the men's tent but is chased away. He tries to sleep in the snow but finds it intolerably cold. He wanders among the tents, but every place is as cold as the last. He feels something wriggling beneath his feet and finds Billee lying in a snug ball, buried warmly under a layer of snow. He digs a hole for himself and sleeps comfortably.

The next day, three more dogs are added to the team, making a total of nine. Buck does not mind the work, but he is surprised that the other dogs seem to enjoy it so wholeheartedly. He is placed between Dave and Sol-leks to receive instruction from them. Francois and Perrault, who are mail carriers for the Canadian government, leave the coast and set out for the town of Dawson. The team makes good time, traveling forty miles in a day. Past the already packed trail, the team moves more slowly for many days, and the men are always setting up camp after dark. Buck is always hungry and learns to eat faster in order to keep his food from disappearing into the mouths of the other dogs. By watching the other dogs, he also learns to steal; his old morals, learned in Judge Miller's sunny home, gradually slip away. Old urges and instincts, which belonged to his wild ancestors, begin to assert themselves.

ANALYSIS

The death of Curly is an important symbolic moment in the novel. In the previous chapter, the man with the club stood for the savage relationship between humans and their dogs; Curly's fate here shows that this savagery also exists among the dogs themselves in the wild North. Cruelty and violence replace friendliness and peaceful coexistence, and any animal that cannot stand up for itself will be killed mercilessly. "So that was the way," Buck realizes. "No fair play." Fair play is the law of civilization; in the wilderness, the only law is the "law of club and fang." Curly's death symbolizes the transition to this new, harsher law of life.

Throughout this chapter, Buck begins to adjust to the new ethic, which requires intense self-reliance. The old Buck is a creature of civilization, one who would die "for a moral consideration"; the new Buck is more than willing to steal food from his masters. His transformation reflects the influence of Darwinian natural science and philosophy on Jack London's novel. Charles Darwin, whose 1859 book *The Origin of Species* proposed the theory of evolution to explain the development of life on Earth, envisioned a natural world defined by fierce competition for scarce resources—"the survival of the fittest" was the law of life and the engine that drove the evolutionary process. In *The Call of the Wild,* Buck must adjust to this bleak, cruel vision of animal existence as he realizes that the moral concerns of human civilization have no place in the kill-or-be-killed world of the wild. What order does exist in this world is instead the order of the pack, which we observe in the way the other members of the team help train Buck as a sled dog. Even within the pack rivalry surfaces, however, as the emerging antagonism between Spitz and Buck demonstrates.

But London emphasizes that Buck does not merely learn these Darwinian lessons; they are already part of his deep animal memory. Buck may be a creature reared in the comfort of the sunny Santa Clara Valley, a domestic pet and a descendant of domestic pets, but his species roamed wild long before men tamed it. As the novel progresses, Buck taps into this ancestral memory and uncovers hidden primal instincts for competition and survival. The term for this process is *atavism*—the reappearance in an animal of the traits that defined its remote ancestors. Atavism is the key to Buck's success in the wild—he is able to access "in vague ways . . . the youth of the breed . . . the time the wild dogs ranged in packs through the primeval forest, and killed their meat as they ran it down." London suggests that primitive instincts do not die in the civilized world; rather, they go into a kind of hibernation. Such a reawakening of instincts certainly occurs in dogs, but the novel suggests that it also occurs in men. Given the right circumstances, any being can return, like Buck, to the primitive, instinctual life of his ancestors.

CHAPTER III: *THE DOMINANT PRIMORDIAL BEAST*

SUMMARY

> *Buck stood and looked on, the successful champion,*
> *the dominant primordial beast who had made his kill*
> *and found it good.*
>
> (See QUOTATIONS, p. 42)

Buck turns to his primitive instincts more and more as he struggles to survive in the wild North. He avoids fights, but Spitz becomes a dangerous rival, showing his teeth whenever possible. One night, Buck settles down under the shelter of a rock, but when he goes to get his food, he finds the space occupied by Spitz. He springs upon Spitz, surprising him, and the two circle each other, preparing to fight, while Francois eggs Buck on. Just then, they hear Perrault shouting and see almost a hundred starving huskies charging into the camp. The wild dogs are so thin that their bones seem to be coming out of their skin, and they are mad with hunger. Buck is attacked by three huskies at once, and his head and shoulders are slashed; even as he fights the wild dogs, Spitz continues to nip at him. Eventually, outnumbered, the sled dogs run out onto the frozen lake and regroup in the woods. They are all badly hurt. In the morning, they make their way back to the camp but find no food there. Surveying the damage, Francois worries that the wild dogs were mad and that their bites may have infected the sled dogs, but Perrault doubts it.

Four hundred miles of trail remain, and the team reaches the most difficult stretch—frozen lakes and rivers where the surface is partially melted. At times they take great risks, and many of the dogs break through the ice and almost freeze to death or drown. Dolly, one of the dogs, goes mad one morning and begins chasing Buck. Francois kills the mad dog with an ax, and Buck is left exhausted from running. Spitz springs on him, but Francois attacks him with his whip. From then on, Buck and Spitz remain rivals engaged in an undeclared war. A fight to the death seems inevitable. Even Francois and Perrault realize it, with Francois betting on Buck and Perrault on Spitz. Before they reach Dawson, Buck threatens Spitz's leadership by siding with the weaker dogs when Spitz tries to bring them into line. But no opportunity for a fight presents itself, and they arrive in the town with the outcome of the struggle still uncertain.

After a brief stopover in Dawson, the team pushes on toward Skaguay, with Buck's insurrection against Spitz growing every day. One night the team spots a rabbit, and fifty dogs from the Northwest Police camp join in the hunt. Buck leads the pack, but Spitz, unbeknownst to Buck, leaves the pack and cuts across a narrow piece of land. Buck thinks that he will catch the rabbit but then sees Spitz cut him off. As Spitz's jaw clamps down on the rabbit's back, Buck drives into Spitz, and the two roll over and over in the snow. Buck realizes that they are locked in a battle to the death. Spitz is a practiced fighter and fends off Buck's attacks patiently. After a few minutes, Buck is dripping with blood, while Spitz is virtually untouched. Spitz begins to rush him, but Buck tricks his rival, faking a rush against the other dog's shoulder and then diving for the leg, instead, and breaking it. Crippled, Spitz soon goes down and, as the other dogs gather to watch, Buck finishes him off.

ANALYSIS

This chapter emphasizes the external dangers of the wild. Life within the world of gold rush towns and sled teams can be dangerous enough, as Curly's death and Buck's rivalry with Spitz demonstrate. But worse threats lurk beyond the confines of camps and mail routes—wild dogs, for one thing, and madness, for another. Hunger also threatens, a terrible enemy that has transformed the wild dogs into weird, skeletal, half-mad creatures. At this point, hunger is not a direct threat to Buck, since Francois and Perrault are responsible masters. But later in the novel, when Buck is in the care of less experienced humans, it rears its head again, and the image of the starving wild dogs foreshadows Buck's later experience with hunger.

Meanwhile, the competition between Buck and Spitz, in which each strives to be "the dominant primordial beast," builds to a climactic resolution. In the Buck-Spitz war, we see again the way that London's dogs resemble humans: Buck's revolt against Spitz is first of all a matter of strength versus strength, but it is also *political*. Buck does not merely attack Spitz head-on; instead, he slyly undercuts Spitz's authority among the other dogs by siding with the weaker animals in disputes. Thus, he paves the way for his own leadership even before the final confrontation arrives.

While Darwinism clearly influenced London's writing, the Buck-Spitz conflict seems to be more suggestive of the ideas of Friedrich Nietzsche—a German philosopher of the late nineteenth century.

Nietzsche argued that all of society was divided up into those who were naturally masters and those who were naturally slaves. Nietzsche further argued that life was a constant struggle either to rule or be ruled; the "will to power," as he termed it, replaced a conventional system of morality or ethics. He frequently resorted to animal metaphors, referring to the conquering rulers as "birds of prey" and "blonde beasts," and to their victims as "sheep" and "herd animals." In *The Call of the Wild,* London transposes Nietzsche's arguments about human competition to dogs in the Klondike, casting Buck as the dominant beast whose "will to power" is unmatched. His language is almost self-consciously Nietzschean: he refers to Buck as a "masterful dog," filled with "pride" and looking forward to a "clash for leadership" because such a desire is in his "nature."

This chapter leaves civilized morality ("slave morality," as Nietzsche called it) far behind. Earlier, the killing of Curly horrifies Buck, whose life in California has left him unprepared to live by a new and different set of moral principles. The demands of the wild, however, force him to reconsider his scruples to the extent that he not only fights and kills Spitz but also rejoices in doing so. The story does not criticize the new, savage Buck; instead, it applauds his victory, his conquest of Spitz, and his assumption of his destiny to rule the pack alone and defeat anyone who opposes him.

CHAPTER IV: *WHO HAS WON TO MASTERSHIP*

SUMMARY

The next morning, Perrault discovers Spitz missing and Buck covered with wounds. The dog-driver harnesses the dogs. Buck trots over to the space Spitz used to occupy, but Francois does not notice him and harnesses Sol-leks to the lead position. Buck lunges at Sol-leks, but Francois drags him away by the scruff of the neck. Sol-leks shows that he is afraid of Buck and does not mind giving up the position, but Francois comes back with the club. Buck retreats but then refuses to take his old position—he is making it clear, Francois realizes, that he thinks that he has earned the lead position and will be satisfied with nothing less.

Perrault tells Francois to throw down his club, and Buck trots to the lead position and is harnessed in. He takes up the job easily and shows himself to be superior even to Spitz. He is a born leader and excels at making the others live up to his expectations. Two native huskies are added to the team, and Buck breaks them in quickly. The team, at this point, is ahead of their record, and they cover the Thirty Mile River in one day, even though it took them ten days to cross before. Averaging forty miles a day, they reach Skaguay in record time, a remarkable journey that makes them extremely popular for a short while.

However, Perrault and Francois soon receive official orders that take them elsewhere, and they exit from Buck's life. The team then travels back to Dawson under the command of a Scotsman, carrying a heavy load of mail to the gold miners in the North. With such a load, their speed slows, and life becomes monotonous and laborious for Buck. Occasionally, he thinks about his life in California, but he is not homesick. His inherited instincts are growing stronger within him, and everything he encounters in the wild seems strangely familiar. The men he is with remind him of men from another, more primitive time, and sometimes at night he has visions that seem to come from an earlier era, when men wore animal skins and lived in caves.

The dogs are tired when they reach Dawson, but they are allowed little rest and are soon on their way out with another load. They are treated well, attended to even before the men. However, one of the dogs, Dave, is suffering from a strange illness that no one can diagnose. The men decide he is too weak to pull the sled and try to pull him out of his position, but he protests until they put him back into his rightful place. They realize that he wants to die working and harness him into his usual position. The next day, he is too weak to travel. He tries to crawl into his position but collapses on the ground and howls mournfully as the team moves away. The Scotsman retraces his steps, the dogs hear a shot ring out, and London writes that "Buck knew, and every dog knew, what had taken place behind the belt of river trees."

ANALYSIS

Buck's victory over Spitz marks his ascendancy within the team of dogs, but the team is not independent—it is subordinate to the orders of human beings, in this case Francois and Perrault. It is not enough for Buck to have killed Spitz; his human masters must ratify his triumph. But having "won to mastery" over Spitz, Buck is not content to passively accept his masters' orders, even when they are accompanied by the use of the club. He has learned from his previous encounters with weapons, and he stays out of range until Francois and Perrault give in and accept what Buck has already proved in slaying Spitz—that he deserves to be the lead dog. Once they do accept this fact, Buck rewards them by raising the team's performance to new heights. The significance of the speed record that they set on the road to Skaguay is clear: not only is Buck the strongest and fiercest dog, but he is also a born leader. Of course, Buck was actually raised as a pet, and, therefore, the irony of his natural capacity for leadership supports the novel's idea that beings innately possess such ancestral traits.

Little transpires in terms of plot development in this chapter: the team travels to Skaguay, then back to Dawson, and then onward almost without incident—except for the change in drivers and the increasing heaviness of the load. The touching death of Dave is both a reminder of the harshness of life in the Klondike and an expression of canine resolution. Even when he is on the brink of death, Dave demands his rightful place in the team and refuses to be unharnessed. He clearly wants to die on his feet, and, while he may not be as mighty and masterful as Buck, he shares the sense of pride that drives Buck to excel and, thus, hangs on for dear life. Dave's exhibition of pride even when all of his bodily strength is gone exemplifies how London has endowed the sled dogs with human emotions.

Meanwhile, London continues to develop the idea of the existence of a kind of species memory, which allows Buck to tap into the experiences of his wild ancestors. This species memory shows itself not only in the instincts that life in the wild has awakened in Buck but also in the visions that Buck begins to have. London makes Buck something of a mystic, able to look into the ancient past, before civilization appeared on the earth. There, he has visions of primeval man, "all but naked . . . afraid of the darkness . . . [with] a quick alertness as of one who lived in perpetual fear of things seen and unseen." With such visions, London suggests that while Buck's life as a pet, in sunny California, may have been soft and overcivilized, the relationship between man and canine stretches back into the primitive world, when humans needed dogs to protect them from the terrors of the night. This idea of an ancient, natural relationship between men and dogs is developed further when Buck acquires the ultimate good master in John Thornton.

CHAPTER V: *THE TOIL OF*
TRACE AND TRAIL

SUMMARY & ANALYSIS

SUMMARY

Thirty days later, the dogs and men arrive back at Skaguay, exhausted and worn down. The drivers expect a long stopover in the town, but they are ordered to deliver more mail right away. The dogs are replaced with a fresh team, and Buck and his mates are sold to two men recently arrived from the States. The new owners, Hal and Charles, are less organized and professional than the previous drivers; Hal carries a knife and a heavy gun, but they are obviously inexperienced and out of place in the Northland.

They load up the sled together with Charles's wife, Mercedes, a spoiled, pampered woman who is also Hal's sister. Laden with all their possessions—pots and pans, clothes and tents—the sled is too heavy to be pulled. Hal tries to whip the team, but the dogs still cannot pull the sled, even when Mercedes pleads with them to pull so that her brother will stop whipping them. An onlooker tells them to break out the frozen runners, and this time the sled moves ahead; but as they hit a steep slope, half the load slips off. Angry, Buck keeps running, with the other dogs following his lead.

Friendly townspeople help collect the goods and the dogs and advise Hal to carry less stuff and get more dogs. The load is cut in half but remains heavy. Charles and Hal buy six more dogs, but the new animals are inexperienced. Buck is generally unhappy with these new owners, who are lazy and sloppy. They travel much more slowly than they expected, because of the owners' disorganization and Mercedes' demands. To make matters worse, they overfeed the dogs at first, then underfeed them when they realize that they are running out of food. One dog, already injured, dies quickly when the food begins to run out, and the new dogs, weak and unused to the North, all begin to starve. Hal, Charles, and Mercedes squabble among themselves and show little compassion for the animals. Mercedes, in particular, constantly picks fights with the men and insists on riding the sled, increasing the weight and making them travel much more slowly.

At the Five Fingers, a stop along the route to Dawson, the dog food runs out, and the dog owners feed their team horsehide instead of meat. Buck pulls as long as he can and then falls down until the whip or club makes him pull again. He has wasted away from starvation and exhaustion, as have his fellows, who drop quickly. The new dogs die, and so does Billee. Soon only five dogs remain alive in the team, and these five are close to starvation. Meanwhile, spring-time has come to the region, and all around them the snow and ice begins to melt.

Eventually, the team reaches John Thornton's camp, where Thornton, an experienced gold hunter, tells them that the ice is melt-ing and that they cannot push on without risking falling through. Hal ignores him and forces the dogs back into harness by whipping them cruelly. Buck, however, refuses to get up, sensing disaster lurk-ing ahead on the trail, even as blows come from Hal's whip and club. Near death, he has stopped feeling any pain. Suddenly, Thorn-ton—who has been watching the entire display—leaps up, pushes Hal back, and stands over Buck, threatening to kill Hal if he strikes the dog again. Hal pulls out his knife, but Thornton knocks it from his hand with the handle of an ax. He cuts Buck out of his traces, and the rest of the team staggers on, dragging the sled across the snow.

John looks Buck over, checking for broken bones, but finds him simply exhausted, starved, and bruised. They watch the sled crawl over the ice. A quarter of a mile away, they suddenly see its back end drop down and hear Mercedes scream. Charles turns to run back, but then a section of ice gives way and the whole sled, dogs and humans included, drops down and disappears into the dark water.

Analysis

Hal, Charles, and Mercedes demonstrate one way that civilization can be more harrowing than wilderness. So far, in the wild North, Buck has been blessed with experienced and sometimes even kind masters. With this trio, however, he experiences the dark side of the human-dog relationship. But the three newcomers are more than simply representative "bad masters." Through the three characters, London exposes the worst side of civilization: its vanity, foolish-ness, stubbornness, and self-absorption along with a cosmopolitan idiocy that is uninformed by the wisdom of the wild.

From their first appearance, Hal, Charles, and Mercedes are pre-sented as stereotypical "greenhorns"—newcomers in a frontier world and woefully out of place. Where the dog-breaker needed only a club to train Buck, Hal carries both a gun and a huge knife. Neither of these items do him any good, since one is traded for much-needed food on the trail, and Thornton easily knocks the other out of his hand during their confrontation. Both Hal and Charles, London writes, possess "a callowness sheer and unutterable." They are absurd figures, and the addition of the whining, spoiled Mercedes only makes matters worse. She and Curly are the only female characters in the book, and neither lasts long. Their early demises may be London's way of suggesting that women are ill-suited for primitive life; it is also possible that London is arguing that culture, by cultivating an ideal of helplessness, denies women the possibility of fully developing their potential. "It was her custom to be helpless," he writes of Mercedes, and such helplessness has no place in the Arctic.

In another place, this trio would be merely absurd, with their constant bickering over various family grudges and general incompetence. But in the wild, incompetence proves deadly. When Hal and Charles wrongly calculate how much food they need by egregiously underestimating the time it will take to reach Dawson, their mistake has devastating consequences for themselves and especially for Buck and the other dogs. Their miscalculation causes the dark side of the human-animal relationship to manifest itself—Buck may be a Nietzschean superman of a dog, but he is still dependent on the wisdom of his human masters. Similarly, Arctic travel, for Mercedes and her men, is "a reality too harsh for their manhood and womanhood." Because of the trio's weakness, the dogs begin to starve, and this chapter, aptly titled "The Toil of Trace and Trail," lingers over the horror of their journey, as most of them die and Buck is reduced to a bruised wreck of his former self. Yet, even in this extremity, London reminds us of his protagonist's indomitable spirit. "It was heartbreaking," he writes, "only Buck's heart was unbreakable."

Still, Buck's dying body requires a savior, which appears in the form of John Thornton. Whereas Hal, Charles, and Mercedes are creatures of comfort and civilization, Thornton is a man of the wild country, with all the wisdom of the North at his disposal. Aware of the dangers, Thornton urges the dog owners to halt; Hal, entirely unaware of these dangers, insists that they must go on. Only Buck escapes the final disaster, both because his strong spirit defies Charles and because his connection to the primitive world allows him to sense impending doom. But he still needs Thornton to save him; he has suffered through the worst that humanity has to offer, but he is not yet ready, or physically strong enough, to break with mankind and go into the true wild.

CHAPTER VI: *FOR THE LOVE OF A MAN*

SUMMARY

*Deep in the forest a call was sounding, and . . . he felt
compelled to turn his back upon the fire, and to
plunge into the forest.*

(See QUOTATIONS, p. 43)

Buck slowly gets his strength back. John Thornton, it turns out, had
frozen his feet during the previous winter, and he and his dogs are
now waiting for the river to melt and for a raft to take them down to
Dawson. With Thornton, Buck experiences love for the first time,
developing a strong affection for the man who saved his life and
who proves an ideal master. Thornton treats his dogs as if they are
his own children, and Buck responds with adoration and obeys all
commands. Once, to test Buck, Thornton tells him to jump off a
cliff; Buck begins to obey before Thornton stops him.

Even though Buck is happy with Thornton, his wild instincts still
remain strong, and he fights as fiercely as ever. Now, however, he
fights in defense of Thornton. In Dawson, Thornton steps in to stop
a fight in a bar, and one of the combatants lashes out at him. Immediately, Buck hurls himself at the man's throat; the man narrowly
escapes having his throat ripped open when he throws up his hand,
though Buck succeeds in partially ripping it open with his second
try. A meeting is called on the spot to decide what to do with Buck,
and the miners rule that his aggressive behavior was justified, since
he acted in defense of Thornton. Soon, Buck has earned a reputation
throughout Alaska for loyalty and fercocity.

Buck saves Thornton's life again when Thornton is thrown out
of a boat and gets caught in fierce rapids. Buck swims to the slick
rock where Thornton clings for his life, and the other men attach a
rope to Buck's neck and shoulders. After several failed attempts,
Thornton grabs onto his neck, and the two are pulled back to safety.

That winter, on a strange whim, Thornton boasts that Buck can
start a sled with a thousand pounds loaded on it. Other men chal-
lenge his claim, betting that Buck cannot perform that task before
their eyes. A man named Matthewson, who has grown rich in the
gold rush, bets a thousand dollars that Buck cannot pull his sled—
which is outside, loaded with a thousand pounds of flour. Thornton
himself doubts it, but he makes the bet anyway, borrowing the

money from a friend to cover the wager. Several hundred men come to watch, giving odds—first two to one, then three to one when the terms of the bet are clarified—that Buck cannot break out the sled, and a confident Matthewson throws on another $600 at those odds. Once Buck is harnessed in, he first breaks the sled free of the ice, then pulls it a hundred yards. The crowd of men cheers in amazement, with even Matthewson joining in the applause.

ANALYSIS

For the time being, Buck's slowly developing identity as a wild animal is quelled by his new devotion to John Thornton and, through him, to the man-dog relationship. If the terrible trio of Hal, Charles, and Mercedes comprises the worst master possible for an animal, then Thornton may be the best. His relationship with Buck is founded on mutual protection and affection—he saves Buck's life, and then Buck not only does the same for him, but also bears out Thornton's faith in him by winning a seemingly impossible wager. This is the first time, London emphasizes, that Buck has actually felt love for a human being—perhaps because it is the first time that he is neither a pampered pet nor a drudge, toiling away to pull a sled. Whatever the cause, this love is presented as being profoundly physical—Thornton shakes him and wrestles with him, and Buck has a way of biting his master's hand that, without drawing blood, is strong enough to leave the marks of his teeth in Thornton's flesh.

Thornton's relationship to Buck seems to be the fulfillment of Buck's mystical vision of primitive man, a vision that recurs in Chapter VII. The relationship of man to dog, the novel suggests, is not a creation of civilization—rather, it is a much more primal bond that can survive even in a dog like Buck, whose civilized veneer is almost entirely scraped away to expose the wild animal beneath. Buck is no longer a pet or a slave, but he still has a master. He has not yet become an animal of the wild.

London also uses this chapter to set the stage for Buck's eventual break with the world of men by telling us that this love for Thornton is the only thing that keeps Buck from going wild. Buck remains merciless, for one thing, holding on to the lessons that he learned from Curly's death and from his war with Spitz—namely, that "he must master or be mastered." His love for Thornton coexists with his knowledge that "kill or be killed, eat or be eaten, was the law." His ability to still feel love is significant and suggests that London is not content with the bleakness of a Darwinian cosmos or with the pure cruelty and struggle for mastery of a Nietzschean worldview. But while Buck's love is strong, it is for Thornton alone and not for mankind in general; he has learned well, especially from Hal and Charles, that mankind at large does not deserve his love. "Thornton alone held him," London writes, and then describes how Buck ranges away from the fire and senses a "call" beckoning him into the deep forests and wilderness. For the time being, Buck resists this call for Thornton's sake, but we are left to wonder what will happen if and when he and Thornton separate. Thus, Buck stands poised on the brink of a final break with the world of men, and the stage is set for the developments of the final chapter.

CHAPTER VII: *THE SOUNDING OF THE CALL*

SUMMARY & ANALYSIS

SUMMARY

John Thornton pays off his debts with money he earns from the bet, and he sets off to the east to find a fabled lost mine that is supposed to make a man rich. Together with his other dogs and his friends Pete and Hans, he and Buck wander in the wilderness, hunting and fishing and living off the land, until they reach a shallow place in a valley full of gold. The men earn thousands of dollars a day panning for gold, and the dogs have nothing to do. Buck begins to feel wild yearnings. One night, he springs up from sleep with a start, hearing a call from the forest. He dashes through the woods and finds a timber wolf, one-third his size. Buck begins to circle the wolf and make friendly advances, but the wolf is afraid.

Finally, the two show their friendship by sniffing noses, and the wolf leads Buck away through the forest. They stop to drink, and Buck remembers John Thornton. The wolf encourages him to keep following, but Buck starts back toward the camp. When he arrives, Thornton is eating dinner, and Buck showers him with affection. For two days, he never allows Thornton out of his sight. Then, he hears the call more loudly than ever and is haunted by recollections of his wild friend. He begins to stay away from the camp for days at a time, hunting his own food.

Buck has two identities at this point: one as sled dog in Thornton's camp, another as wild hunter in the forest. He kills a bear and fishes for salmon the river; when the moose come in the fall, Buck hunts them eagerly. He cuts a bull away from the pack to kill him and finally brings him down after four days. Then he heads back to the camp. On the way, he feels a strange stirring in the wilderness, of something new abroad, and he feels a premonition of calamity. His feeling is proven correct when he finds Thornton's dog Nig and one of the dogs bought in Dawson, both dying on the trail. As he approaches the camp, he sees Hans lying facedown, arrows covering him. He peers out to where the lodge had been and sees Yeehat Indians dancing in the wreckage. Buck charges, cutting their throats with his fangs and killing several of them. The Indians scatter, and Buck finds the rest of his camp, including Thornton, dead.

Buck mourns his dead master but feels pride at having killed the Yeehats. Henceforth, he will not fear men unless they carry weapons. He hears the call of the wolf again. His ties to Thornton broken by death, he heads off to follow it. He finds the pack, and one wolf lunges for his throat, but he breaks its neck easily. Three others try but pull back. After half an hour they all draw back, and one of them approaches Buck in a friendly manner. Buck recognizes him to be the wolf he encountered in the woods. Buck joins the wolf pack, and the Yeehats notice a difference in the local breed of timber wolves as years pass. They also tell of a Ghost Dog that runs at the front of the pack, singing songs and leaping above his fellows. They tell of a haunted valley—where Thornton lies dead—where an evil spirit dwells, and where, every year, Buck comes and mourns for a time beside the stream before loping away to rejoin the pack.

ANALYSIS

Early in this chapter, Buck's vision of primitive man recurs, and this time, he sees himself running alongside the "hairy man," hunting with him in the forest, and guarding him while he sleeps. In these images, London once again emphasizes the primitive nature of the man-dog relationship and the strength of the bond that ties Buck to John Thornton. But the bond is constantly tested by the equally strong call that draws Buck away from human life and deeper into the wilderness—a call that fills Buck with "a great unrest and strange desires." As Thornton and his friends sift for gold in the wild, Buck's soul is in a state of extreme tension, torn between his loyalty to his master and his destiny as a wild animal.

His encounter with the timber wolf, whose smallness reminds us of Buck's remarkable size and power, is an important step in his development as a wild creature, since it offers the promise of a community of wild creatures. Buck need not be alone in the wild; he can find companionship not only from humans and dogs but also in the tight-knit world of the pack. Meanwhile, Buck's long hunt of the moose enables London to emphasize the importance of what he terms "blood-longing" in Buck; once again, the novel emphasizes the kill-or-be-killed nature of life in the wild and shows us how Buck, the "dominant primordial beast," is the ultimate killer. "He was a killer," the novel insists, "a thing that preyed, living on the things that lived, unaided, alone, by virtue of his own strength and prowess, surviving triumphantly in a hostile environment where only the strong survive." These sentiments are the language of Darwin and Nietzsche, portraying life as an unceasing struggle for survival in which only the strong—only the Bucks of the world—can last for long.

Still, it takes Thornton's death to enable Buck to enter this wild world fully. For the first time in the novel, he has no master: he has been passed from Judge Miller to the dog traders to Francois to Hal and finally to Thornton. But Thornton's death ends the succession of masters and leaves him the master of his own fate. The only humans that remain in his world are the Yeehats, and Buck scatters them, triumphantly demonstrating that he is the master, not they. His attack on them marks the final step in his escape from the world of men. Earlier, he learns that humans can be violent, like the man who beats him with the club, and foolish, like Hal, Charles, and Mercedes. After all that has happened in the North, he learns he can kill men at will. The last traces of the old, civilized morality vanish, and Judge Miller's Buck, who would die for a principle, is transformed into a beast who kills with impunity and without remorse.

London treats this transformation as triumph, not tragedy. Morality functions well in the civilized world, the novel suggests, but Buck's authentic, animal nature is amoral—it obeys the law of the wild, in which brute strength is the only arbiter of justice. This strength wins the respect of the wolves, who first fight Buck and then obey him; and this strength makes him a legend among the Yeehats. When the novel opens, Buck is a king, but a soft monarch ruling a gentle land obtained only by his birthright. As the novel closes, he is a king again, but his kingdom is a very different place from Judge Miller's warm Santa Clara spread. More important, he has won his kingdom by his own efforts and nothing else. He is a self-made monarch, having faced a cruel, uncaring world—and mastered it.

IMPORTANT QUOTATIONS EXPLAINED

1. During the four years since his puppyhood he had lived the life of a sated aristocrat; he had a fine pride in himself, was even a trifle egotistical, as country gentlemen sometimes become because of their insular situation.

This quotation is from the beginning of Chapter 1, "Into the Primitive," and it defines Buck's life before he is kidnapped and dragged into the harsh world of the Klondike. As a favored pet on Judge Miller's sprawling California estate, Buck lives like a king—or at least like an "aristocrat" or a "country gentleman," as London describes him. In the civilized world, Buck is born to rule, only to be ripped from this environment and forced to fight for his survival. The story of *The Call of the Wild* is, in large part, the story of Buck's climb back to the top after his early fall from grace. He loses one kind of lordship, the "insular" and "sated" lordship into which he is born, but he gains a more authentic kind of mastery in the wild, one that he wins by his own efforts rather than by an accident of birth.

2. He was beaten (he knew that); but he was not broken.
    He saw, once for all, that he stood no chance against a
    man with a club. He had learned the lesson, and in all
    his after life he never forgot it. That club was a
    revelation. It was his introduction to the reign of
    primitive law, and he met the introduction halfway.
    The facts of life took on a fiercer aspect and, while he
    faced that aspect uncowed, he faced it with all the
    latent cunning of his nature aroused.

This quotation is taken from late in Chapter 1, "Into the Primitive," just after Buck has been beaten repeatedly by one of his kidnappers. Each time he is clubbed, Buck leaps up to attack again, until finally the man knocks him unconscious. This incident is Buck's introduction to a new way of life, vastly different from the pampered existence that he led in the Santa Clara Valley. There, civilized law, and civilized morality were the ruling forces—symbolized by the fact that his first master, Judge Miller, is a *judge*. In the wild, though, Buck comes to terms with "the reign of primitive law," in which might makes right, and a man with a club (or a powerful dog) can do as he pleases to weaker creatures. In this scene, Buck is mastered by the man with the club, but he learns his lesson well and soon comes to master others.

3.   And not only did he learn by experience, but instincts long dead became alive again. The domesticated generations fell from him. In vague ways he remembered back to the youth of the breed, to the time the wild dogs ranged in packs through the primeval forest and killed their meat as they ran it down. . . . Thus, as token of what a puppet thing life is the ancient song surged through him and he came into his own again. . . .

This quote, taken from Chapter II, shows that as Buck fights for survival in the harsh world of the Klondike, he relies increasingly on buried instincts that belonged to his wild forebears. The role of this atavistic development—"atavism" refers to the recovery by an animal of behaviors that belonged to its ancestors—points to one of the central themes of London's novel, namely, the way that primitive instincts and urges persist beneath the veneer of civilization. Throw a soft, civilized creature (human or animal) into the wild, London suggests, and if he survives, he, like Buck, will come to depend on the same instincts that guided the life of his primitive ancestors. "The ancient song," in his phrase, is only waiting for the right opportunity to emerge.

QUOTATIONS

4.   A pause seemed to fall. Every animal was motionless
     as though turned to stone. Only Spitz quivered and
     bristled as he staggered back and forth, snarling with
     horrible menace, as though to frighten off impending
     death. Then Buck sprang in and out; but while he was
     in, shoulder had at last squarely met shoulder. The
     dark circle became a dot on the moon-flooded snow
     as Spitz disappeared from view. Buck stood and
     looked on, the successful champion, the dominant
     primordial beast who had made his kill and found it
     good.

These words constitute the final paragraph in Chapter III, describ-
ing the climactic battle between Buck and Spitz. The paragraph
marks the moment that Buck comes into his own by vanquishing
and killing his great rival, and then taking Spitz's place as the team's
lead dog. He has left his life as a pampered pet far behind—now he
is "the successful champion . . . the dominant primordial beast."
Throughout the novel, London suggests that life in the wild is
defined by a struggle for mastery, and the Buck-Spitz duel is the central example of this struggle, the moment when Buck establishes
himself as a master of the kill-or-be-killed ethic of the wild.

5. [Each] day mankind and the claims of mankind
   slipped farther from him. Deep in the forest a call was
   sounding, and as often as he heard this call,
   mysteriously thrilling and luring, he felt compelled to
   turn his back upon the fire, and to plunge into the
   forest. . . . But as often as he gained the soft unbroken
   earth and the green shade, the love of John Thornton
   drew him back to the fire again.

This quotation is from Chapter vi, "For the Love of a Man," and it
depicts the tension building within Buck during his time with John
Thornton. Thornton is the ideal master, and his relationship with
Buck represents a perfect partnership between man and dog. London tells us that this is the first time that Buck has truly loved a
human being. Yet, at the same time, it is clear that Buck's destiny lies
in the wild, and so he is torn between the urges that pull him away
from humanity and his intense loyalty to Thornton. That love, it
becomes clear, is the only thing tying him to the world of men—
which means that when Thornton is killed, there is nothing left to
hold him, and he embraces his destiny as a wild creature.

QUOTATIONS

KEY FACTS

FULL TITLE
The Call of the Wild

AUTHOR
Jack London

TYPE OF WORK
Novel

GENRE
Dog story; adventure story

LANGUAGE
English

TIME AND PLACE WRITTEN
1903, California

DATE OF FIRST PUBLICATION
Serialized in *The Saturday Evening Post,* June 20–July 18, 1903

PUBLISHER
The Saturday Evening Post

NARRATOR
Anonymous, speaking from a point in time after the events in the novel have taken place

POINT OF VIEW
Buck's point of view, for the most part; the novel also shifts briefly into John Thornton's point of view during his wager involving Buck's ability to pull a heavy sled

TONE
Sweeping, romantic, heroic

TENSE
Past

SETTING (TIME)
The late 1890s

SETTING (PLACE)
California, briefly; then Alaska and the Klondike region of Canada

PROTAGONIST
Buck

MAJOR CONFLICT
Buck's struggle against his masters and his development from a tame dog into a wild beast

RISING ACTION
Buck's battle with Spitz; Buck's struggle with Hal, Charles, and Mercedes; Buck's fulfillment of Thornton's wager

CLIMAX
John Thornton's saving of Buck's life from Hal's cruelty

FALLING ACTION
Buck's time with Thornton, leading up to Thornton's death

THEMES
The laws of civilization and of wilderness; the membership of the individual in the group; the power of instinct and ancestral memory; the struggle for mastery

MOTIFS
Fights to the death; visions

SYMBOLS
Mercedes' possessions symbolize the different meanings of objects in the civilized and uncivilized worlds; Buck's traces symbolize, variously, his entrance into the wild, his superiority over the other animals, and, finally, his breaking free from the group. The club that breaks Buck in as a pack dog symbolizes the law of the uncivilized world; Curly's death also symbolizes the break with civilization. Buck's killing of the Yeehat Indians symbolizes his final abandonment of life as a tame animal.

FORESHADOWING
The urges that Buck feels pulling him into the wild foreshadow his eventual transformation into a wild creature; the starving dogs who attack the team's camp in Chapter III foreshadow the hunger that will afflict them during their ill-fated journey with Hal, Charles, and Mercedes.

KEY FACTS

STUDY QUESTIONS & ESSAY TOPICS

STUDY QUESTIONS

1. *How does* The Call of the Wild *present the human-dog relationship?*

London's novel is the story of Buck's transformation from a pampered pet to a fierce, masterful wild animal, and this transformation naturally means that the canine protagonist gradually separates himself from his human masters on his way to achieving a final independence. Nevertheless, *The Call of the Wild* ultimately offers an ambiguous, rather than negative, portrait of Buck's relationship to humanity. It suggests that while some human-dog relationships can be disastrous to the dog's welfare, others are mutually beneficial, and a natural love can develop between dogs and their masters. The negative side of the man-dog compact is embodied in Hal, Charles, and Mercedes, whose inexperience, stubbornness, and general incompetence bring disaster not only on themselves but also on their sled dogs. The trio's failure to understand the laws of the wild ultimately leads to the death of every one of their animals—except, of course, Buck, whom John Thornton saves. It is Thornton, whom Buck loves intensely, who embodies the better way in which humans and dogs can be partners, where each looks out for the other's welfare. Buck's visions of primitive man and his faithful dog suggest that this relationship is ultimately more primitive than civilized, and that there may be a natural bond between men and their dogs that predates modern society. Nevertheless, the story ultimately demands that even this bond be cast aside and that Buck seek his own way—suggesting that for the truly masterful animal, the greatest of dogs, having a master is only a temporary condition.

2. *What is the "law of club and fang"? What does it represent? How is Buck introduced to it?*

The opening of the novel sets up a contrast between two worlds: the sunny, comfortable world of Judge Miller's estate, where Buck lives in spoiled, lordly contentment, and the harsh, frigid world of the Klondike, where he is dragged against his will. The judge's world, as his title suggests, is defined by moral and legal codes, while the world of the Klondike is governed by a very different law. In the cold North, might makes right, and one must be willing to fight if one wishes to stay alive. Strength, not justice, is the central value. Buck learns this lesson from two events. First, he is beaten with a club by one of his kidnappers until he learns obedience, an event that teaches him about the power of violence and about the need to give in when threatened by a superior force. This reality constitutes the law of the club, and Buck learns the law of the fang when he arrives in Canada and watches one of his fellow dogs, a female dog named Curly, torn to pieces by a pack of huskies. "So that was the way," he thinks to himself. "No fair play. Once down, that was the end of you." These are the rules that Buck learns to live by and excel at in order to eventually become a king whose rule is defined by the "law of club and fang."

3. *Discuss the influence of Charles Darwin's and Friedrich Nietzsche's theories on* The Call of the Wild.

In writing his novel, Jack London was profoundly influenced by the writings of these two nineteenth-century thinkers. Darwin, the founding father of evolution theory, taught that life in the natural world consisted of a constant struggle for survival, in which only the strong could thrive and produce offspring. This "survival of the fittest," as Herbert Spencer, an English philosopher, termed it, was the engine that drove evolution. The world that London creates in *The Call of the Wild* operates strictly according to Darwinist principles in its brutality and amorality—only the fit survive in the cruel landscape of the Klondike.

Nietzsche was a German philosopher who preached the doctrine of the "will to power" as the driving force behind society. Moral considerations were meaningless, he declared, and all members of humanity were either masters, driven to dominate others, or slaves, driven to submit. London transposes this scheme to the animal world, using Nietzschean language repeatedly to describe Buck's quest to achieve mastery and dominion over his enemies, from Spitz to the animals he hunts in the forest to the Yeehat Indians who kill Thornton. Buck is clearly a canine version of Nietzsche's superman. He is an Alexander the Great among dogs, since his will to power drives him to excel. Similarly, the audience celebrates his victories, not because he is moral but because he is mighty.

SUGGESTED ESSAY TOPICS

1. Discuss Mercedes, Hal, and Charles. What role do they play in the novel? How do they function as embodiments of the worst side of civilization?

2. What is "atavism"? What role does it play in Buck's development as a wild animal?

3. To what extent does London anthropomorphize Buck—that is, present him like a human being? To what extent is he emphatically an animal?

4. Compare the roles of John Thornton and Judge Miller. Who, from the novel's point of view, is the better master? Defend your answer.

5. What is the "call of the wild"? How does it affect Buck's behavior throughout the novel?

REVIEW & RESOURCES

QUIZ

1. What is Buck?

   A. A dog, half St. Bernard and half Scottish shepherd
   B. A young gold hunter
   C. An Arabian stallion
   D. An Alaskan wolf

2. Where does Buck live at the beginning of the novel?

   A. Nome, Alaska
   B. Vermont
   C. The Santa Clara Valley, in California
   D. Flagstaff, Arizona

3. What is the name of Buck's first master?

   A. John Thornton
   B. Judge Miller
   C. Manuel
   D. Mercedes

4. Who kidnaps Buck from his home?

   A. Hal and Charles
   B. Yeehat Indians
   C. Judge Miller
   D. Manuel, a gardener

5. Which dog gets killed immediately upon her arrival in the North?

   A. Curly
   B. Spitz
   C. Mercedes
   D. Koona

6. What is the profession of Francois and Perrault?

    A. Gold hunters
    B. Dog trainers
    C. Mail carriers
    D. Fur traders

7. Who is Buck's great rival on the team of dogs?

    A. Teeka
    B. Spitz
    C. Koona
    D. Sol-leks

8. What event intervenes to stop a fight between Buck and Spitz?

    A. An avalanche
    B. An attack by Indians
    C. A flash flood
    D. An attack by wild dogs

9. What event brings about the final confrontation between Buck and Spitz?

    A. A wild chase after a rabbit
    B. A dispute over some food
    C. A fire in the camp
    D. The death of Billee

10. What does Buck demand after Spitz's death?

    A. More food
    B. Less work
    C. That he be made the lead dog
    D. That he be allowed to run wild

11. Who buys Buck and the other dogs when they are sold by the mail company?

    A. John Thornton
    B. Hal and Charles
    C. Judge Miller
    D. Matthewson

12. What does Mercedes insist on doing that slows the sled down?

    A. Stopping frequently to feed the dogs
    B. Taking shortcuts over patches of dirt
    C. Buying fewer dogs
    D. Riding on the sled herself

13. What happens to the dogs during Hal and Charles's trip to Dawson?

    A. They begin to die of starvation
    B. They make record time
    C. They break their harnesses and escape into the woods
    D. They begin to attack one another

14. How does John Thornton save Buck's life?

    A. He shoots Hal and Charles
    B. He pulls him out of the river when the ice breaks
    C. He prevents Hal from beating him to death
    D. He goes to Dawson to get medicine for Buck's illness

15. What happens to Hal, Charles, and Mercedes after they leave John Thornton's?

    A. They reach Dawson unscathed
    B. Their sled and team breaks through the ice and they drown
    C. They are ambushed by Yeehat Indians
    D. They die of starvation

16. How does Buck save John Thornton's life?

    A. Buck kills a man who is about to shoot Thornton
    B. Buck fends off attacking Yeehat Indians
    C. Buck pulls his master back when Thornton is about to fall off a cliff
    D. When Thornton gets caught in the rapids, Buck swims to him and pulls him to safety

17. What bet does Thornton win with Matthewson?

    A. That Buck can outrun a train
    B. That Buck can move a sled loaded with a thousand pounds
    C. That Buck will do anything Thornton orders him to do
    D. That Buck can find a buried treasure

18. What does Buck do when Thornton gets into a bar fight?

    A. He cowers under the bar
    B. He drags Thornton outside by the collar
    C. He leaps at the throat of Thornton's assailant
    D. He runs to find the police

19. What quest sends Thornton and his friends into the wilderness?

    A. The search for a legendary lost mine
    B. The search for Thornton's missing brother
    C. The search for the Northwest Passage
    D. The search for a lost tribe of Indians

20. While the men camp and look for gold, what does Buck do?

    A. He scouts for hostile Indians
    B. He returns to Dawson carrying messages
    C. He sleeps all day
    D. He spends long periods of time in the deep forest, making contact with wolves

21. What kind of animal does Buck spend four days hunting?

    A. A mountain lion
    B. A moose
    C. A polar bear
    D. A wolf

22. What does Buck find when he returns from hunting?

    A. The camp has burned
    B. John Thornton has abandoned him and returned to Dawson
    C. The camp has been attacked by Yeehat Indians
    D. Nothing is amiss

23. What happens to John Thornton?

    A. He is killed by Indians
    B. He is lost in a blizzard and freezes to death
    C. He dies of hunger
    D. He lives to a ripe old age in Nome

24. What does Buck learn when he attacks the Yeehat Indians?

    A. That they are too strong for him
    B. That he cannot kill humans
    C. That arrows hurt
    D. That he can kill men, as long as they are not armed

25. What does Buck do at the end of the novel?

    A. He drowns
    B. He goes mad and is killed by John Thornton
    C. He is killed by wolves
    D. He joins a wolf pack and becomes a legendary figure in the wild

Answer Key:
1: A; 2: C; 3: B; 4: D; 5: A; 6: C; 7: B; 8: D; 9: A; 10: C; 11: B; 12: D; 13: A; 14: C; 15: B; 16: D; 17: B; 18: C; 19: A; 20: D; 21: B; 22: C; 23: A; 24: D; 25: D

SUGGESTIONS FOR FURTHER READING

KERSHAW, ALEX. *Jack London: A Life*. New York: St. Martin's Press, 1997.

LABOR, EARLE. *Jack London*. New York: Twayne Publishers, 1994.

LONDON, JACK. *The Call of the Wild and White Fang*. London: Bantam Books, 1981.

NUERNBERG, SUSAN M., ed. *The Critical Response to Jack London*. Westport, Connecticut: Greenwood Press, 1994.

TAVERNIER-COURBIN, JACQUELINE. THE CALL OF THE WILD: *A Naturalistic Romance*. New York: Twayne Publishers, 1994.

— — —. *Critical Essays on Jack London*. Boston: G. K. Hall, 1983.

WATSON, CHARLES N. *The Novels of Jack London: A Reappraisal*. Madison: University of Wisconsin Press, 1983.

REVIEW & RESOURCES

SparkNotes
Test Preparation
Guides

The SparkNotes team figured it was time to cut standardized tests down to size. We've studied the tests for you, so that SparkNotes test prep guides are:

Smarter:
Packed with critical-thinking skills and test-
taking strategies that will improve your score.

Better:
Fully up to date, covering all new features of the tests,
with study tips on every type of question.

Faster:
Our books cover exactly what you need to
know for the test. No more, no less.

SparkNotes Guide to the SAT & PSAT
SparkNotes Guide to the SAT & PSAT—Deluxe Internet Edition
SparkNotes Guide to the ACT
SparkNotes Guide to the ACT—Deluxe Internet Edition
SparkNotes Guide to the SAT II Writing
SparkNotes Guide to the SAT II U.S. History
SparkNotes Guide to the SAT II Math Ic
SparkNotes Guide to the SAT II Math IIc
SparkNotes Guide to the SAT II Biology
SparkNotes Guide to the SAT II Physics

SparkNotes Study Guides:

1984

The Adventures of
   Huckleberry Finn

The Adventures of
   Tom Sawyer

The Aeneid

All Quiet on the
   Western Front

And Then There
   Were None

Angela's Ashes

Animal Farm

Anne of Green Gables

Antony and Cleopatra

As I Lay Dying

As You Like It

The Awakening

The Bean Trees

The Bell Jar

Beloved

Beowulf

Billy Budd

Black Boy

Bless Me, Ultima

The Bluest Eye

Brave New World

The Brothers
   Karamazov

The Call of the Wild

Candide

The Canterbury Tales

Catch-22

The Catcher in the Rye

The Chosen

Cold Mountain

Cold Sassy Tree

The Color Purple

The Count of
   Monte Cristo

Crime and Punishment

The Crucible

Cry, the Beloved
   Country

Cyrano de Bergerac

Death of a Salesman

The Diary of a
   Young Girl

Doctor Faustus

A Doll's House

Don Quixote

Dr. Jekyll and Mr. Hyde

Dracula

Dune

Emma

Ethan Frome

Fahrenheit 451

Fallen Angels

A Farewell to Arms

Flowers for Algernon

The Fountainhead

Frankenstein

The Glass Menagerie

Gone With the Wind

The Good Earth

The Grapes of Wrath

Great Expectations

The Great Gatsby

Gulliver's Travels

Hamlet

The Handmaid's Tale

Hard Times

Harry Potter and the
   Sorcerer's Stone

Heart of Darkness

Henry IV, Part I

Henry V

Hiroshima

The Hobbit

The House of the
   Seven Gables

I Know Why the
   Caged Bird Sings

The Iliad

Inferno

Invisible Man

Jane Eyre

Johnny Tremain

The Joy Luck Club

Julius Caesar

The Jungle

The Killer Angels

King Lear

The Last of the
   Mohicans

Les Misérables

A Lesson Before
   Dying

The Little Prince

Little Women

Lord of the Flies

Macbeth

Madame Bovary

A Man for All Seasons

The Mayor of
   Casterbridge

The Merchant of
   Venice

A Midsummer
   Night's Dream

Moby-Dick

Much Ado About
   Nothing

My Ántonia

Mythology

Native Son

The New Testament

Night

The Odyssey

The Oedipus Trilogy

Of Mice and Men

The Old Man and
   the Sea

The Old Testament

Oliver Twist

The Once and
   Future King

One Flew Over the
   Cuckoo's Nest

One Hundred Years
   of Solitude

Othello

Our Town

The Outsiders

Paradise Lost

The Pearl

The Picture of
   Dorian Gray

A Portrait of the Artist
   as a Young Man

Pride and Prejudice

The Prince

A Raisin in the Sun

The Red Badge of
   Courage

The Republic

Richard III

Robinson Crusoe

Romeo and Juliet

The Scarlet Letter

A Separate Peace

Silas Marner

Sir Gawain and the
   Green Knight

Slaughterhouse-Five

Snow Falling on Cedars

The Sound and the Fury

Steppenwolf

The Stranger

A Streetcar Named
   Desire

The Sun Also Rises

A Tale of Two Cities

The Taming of
   the Shrew

The Tempest

Tess of the
   d'Urbervilles

Their Eyes Were
   Watching God

Things Fall Apart

To Kill a Mockingbird

To the Lighthouse

Treasure Island

Twelfth Night

Ulysses

Uncle Tom's Cabin

Walden

Wuthering Heights

A Yellow Raft in
   Blue Water